Christianity

THE WRONGFULLY CONVICTED

James Burchfield

NEW HARBOR PRESS
RAPID CITY, SD

Copyright © 2021 by James Burchfield.

All rights reserved. No part of this publication may be reproduced, distributed or transmitted in any form or by any means, including photocopying, recording, or other electronic or mechanical methods, without the prior written permission of the publisher, except in the case of brief quotations embodied in critical reviews and certain other noncommercial uses permitted by copyright law. For permission requests, write to the publisher, addressed "Attention: Permissions Coordinator," at the address below.

Burchfield/New Harbor Press
1601 Mt. Rushmore Rd, Ste 3288
Rapid City, SD 57701
www.NewHarborPress.com

Ordering Information:
Quantity sales. Special discounts are available on quantity purchases by corporations, associations, and others. For details, contact the "Special Sales Department" at the address above.

Christianity/James Burchfield. -- 1st ed.
ISBN 978-1-63357-252-2

Contributing Editors:
Debra Buettner
Kennedy Green
Jean Camba

Contents

Introduction 1

PART ONE 5

CHAPTER I: THE NEW FRONTIER 7

CHAPTER II: THE INQUISITION 13

CHAPTER III: THE WITCH TRIALS 23

CHAPTER IV: THE CRUSADES 33

CONCLUSION: PART ONE 45

PART TWO 49

CHAPTER V: HINDUISM- The soil Buddhism sprang from 51

CHAPTER VI: THE BEGINNING OF BUDDHISM 57

FINAL CONCLUSION 67

REFERENCES 75

Introduction

My earliest memories are of my mother reading me the bible in the late evenings. I was only a preschooler at that time. Late evening was a good time for reading. Back in the early fifties, there were only two television channels in my area so people did not give themselves to the TV as many do now during their mealtimes.

In my early twenties, I started to tell people I was an atheist. Through considerable soul searching in my forties, I realized that I was never really an atheist. Allow me to explain. Back in my 20's and 30's I would drink scotch on the rocks when actually I hated scotch. I had drunk scotch because people on television shows and movies would order a scotch on the rocks. So, I thought it must be the drink of the rich and sophisticated. I spent nearly two decades drinking something I disliked. Eventually, I came to my senses and switched to beer and an occasional rum and coke. Claiming to be an atheist was for similar reasons. I had it in my head that it was intellectual to be an atheist. It is amazing how superficial a person will be if he is more concerned with image than truth. In those youthful years, I occasionally would read the Bible, I suspect, I was looking for loopholes.

I am not a theologian; however, I have spent the last twenty years studying the bible and have read it more times than I can remember. Once I finish studying it, I go back to the beginning and start over. I find that listening to various preachers helps because sometimes they mention something that suddenly gives some insight. Sometimes, I disagree with the preacher on some points that can not be backed with bible scriptures. Yes, I believe in fact checking everyone.

I started drafting this book because I became weary of people blaming Christianity for many of the atrocities that have occurred throughout history. To mention a few, there was the conquering of the Caribbean and western hemisphere natives and the Spanish Inquisition which was sanctioned by the Roman Catholic Church where many people were tortured and executed. I have only researched four of the atrocities, but it is adequate to draw my conclusions. If a person will take the time to study the New Testament, specifically the quotes from Jesus, they will easily see those atrocities are not the teachings of Christianity. On the contrary, a person would have to conclude that the atrocities are a complete contradiction to Jesus's teaching

I have noticed a steady increase in interest of Buddhism in the United State and elsewhere. Some people that look into Buddhism have mistakenly thought that Christianity was the cause of these forementioned atrocities. I am not writing this in any way to condemn Buddhism but to have a better understanding so as to help me achieve my second goal, which is to understand this ever-increasing growth in Buddhism. I was surprised that many of the core beliefs pertaining to morals and values are similar to beliefs of the Christian faith. (More detail to follow) I feel that to make an opinion on something like Buddhism, I should make a serious study so my decision will be informed. I have two goals. The first goal is to prove that Christianity cannot be blamed for the atrocities and the second goal is to try and understand the growing interest in Buddhism in the western world.

I have spent 8 months of the Covid-19 lockdown researching these subjects and it has given me much pleasure. I can only hope my research can give readers some insights not previously considered. There may be disagreement on some of my conclusions, but I based them on scripture learned from more than 20 years of serious bible study. If I hear a preacher say something that's not familiar, I fact check them with bible scripture. I have made it a point to listen to preachers of different denominations and different preaching styles. I see it as a mysterious puzzle, as I do not have all the pieces. Through serious study God sometimes gives me another piece of the puzzle. I am sure many preachers have more puzzle pieces than me, but I don't believe any of them have all the pieces, therefore I can disagree if I have a puzzle piece (scripture) to support my disagreement.

PART ONE

CHAPTER I

THE NEW FRONTIER

Mathew 10:16 "Behold, I send you forth as sheep in the midst of wolves, therefore be wise as serpents and harmless as doves".

In the 15th century, the trade routes from Europe to India were being controlled by the Ottoman Empire which was not on good terms with Europe. Consequently, in 1492 Columbus was financed to sail and find sea route. Instead of India, Columbus found the Caribbean and the Americas. The lands were rich in minerals and native treasures.

To help justify the atrocities committed by the conquerors, Pope Alexander VI in the year 1493 AD issued a Papal Bull Decree that divided up much of the newly found world between Spain and Portugal. I quote a section of the decree. "We make appoint and depute you and your heirs and successors of them with full and free power, authority, and jurisdiction of every kind."The Pope gave the decree with instructions to Spain to colonize, to convert the natives to Christianity and subject them to be ruled.

The job of conquering was given to the Conquistadors. They were military men who could be compared to generals or other high-ranking military officers. They were to govern the area they conquered. They also received much of the treasures robbed from the natives. The conquest was a slaughter. The Aztec empire fell in 1592 when they were defeated by the Spanish General Hernan Cortes who only had three hundred troops being well outnumbered. However, Cortes was able the get some allies from other tribes. It is estimated that as many as 50% of the indigenous populations died from diseases brought in by the Europeans. Smallpox was especially lethal. In 1531, a different General named Francisco Pizarro conquered the Incas with 200 men. However, some of the tribes continued putting up resistance for decades. The Conquistadors were ruthless during the conquest. In 1992, the Indigenous Land Corporation (ILC) started a process of getting the church to revoke the Papal Bull of 1493. The Institute stated that the military conquest, disease and slavery has caused as many as 100,000,000 deaths in just a few hundred years. Other lands were covered by the Papal Bull besides the area I am referring to. I searched to see if it was revoked and as of Jan 2021 I have yet to discover proof the Catholic church has indeed revoked the decree. If they have revoked it, I have yet to discover it.

The big question is was this brought about by Christianity? I say no and am going to explain why.During this time, people were not allowed to read or own bibles. The church stated that the masses did not have proper instruction to read or understand the bible. The church even made a law against translating it into other languages. The clergy could own bibles but only the Latin Vulgate Translation. So, if you are a layperson and accidentally found a bible, you would need to know Latin. Plus, it would be good to get rid of that bible quickly because people who violated the bible ban were imprisoned, banished, put into forced labor, and sometimes even executed. Naturally, the bibles that were confiscated were destroyed. This ban certainly made it easier for the High Clergy to control people's opinions. The bible ban was enforced by the Church Inquisition, and they were profoundly serious people.

With help from the pope with his decree, it was easy to deceive most people into thinking the Conquistadors were doing God's work by converting the native "heathens" to Christianity. They were "saving their souls." Whereas their real motives were lust for power, influence, and great wealth. I remember hearing several Muslims say that the terrorist did not represent their religion but insisted they had hijacked their religion for their own evil purposes. It is nothing new. Christianity has been hijacked many times throughout history by evil people posing as Christians. It is my objective to clearly prove that point.

Fortunately, I live in a different time and have access to a bible. The scriptures clearly show that the military conquest and conversion of the natives to Christianity was in contradiction to what Jesus Christ taught. **Matthew 10:16** *"Behold, I send you* *forth as sheep in the midst of wolves; be ye therefore wise as serpents, and harmless as doves".* There is no mention of swords in forcing people to convert.

As for wealth, this is what Jesus taught to his Evangelists. **Matthew 10:9-10** *"Provide neither gold nor silver nor brass in your purses, nor scrip for your journey, neither two coats, neither shoes nor yet slaves, for a workman is worthy of his meat".* Please note they were not instructed to acquire wealth in their travels. Instead, they were worthy of their meat. Which I think means necessities such as food. **2 Timothy 2:24** pertains to this saying *"And the servant must not strive, but be gentle unto all men, able to teach, patient".* **John 13:34** further says *"A new commandment I give unto you, that ye love one another; as I have loved you, that ye also love one another"* The bible is a total book of verses that demonstrate the loving, kind, and forgiving nature of Jesus. Christians were taught that we should try our best to follow the examples of Jesus. The works of the Conquistadors, Kings, and Queens of Europe, as well as the Papal Bull of 1493, differed greatly from the Christian values taught by the New Testament. I would, however, like to point out a couple of verses from the Bible. It is written **in 1 Peter 5:8** *"Be sober, be vigilant, because your adversary the devil. As a roaring lion walking about seeking whom he may devour".* **Ephesians 6:12** *"For we wrestle not against flesh and blood, but against principalities, against powers, against the rulers of the darkness of this world, against spiritual wickedness in high places".* With the previous two verses in mind, I would suggest that people fact-check their spiritual leaders and politicians against scripture in the Bible to see if what they say is true Christianity or man-made doctrine.

Basically, the kings and queens of Europe, assisted by the Papal Bull of 1493, were able to convince the masses they were doing the work of God. I am more inclined to believe they were the actions of spiritually wicked people in high places that were mentioned in Ephesians 6:12. As such, Satan was able to create much suffering in the world which would be blamed on Christianity. Sort of a momentary victory for Satan. I do think that even if there was no Papal Bull, Europeans would have invaded the new world to increase their wealth and power. The Papal Bull just helped them to disguise the real motives and use religion to justify their actions.

CHAPTER II

THE INQUISITION

Matthew 15:9 "But in vain they worship me, teaching for doctrine the commandments of man.

The Catholic Inquisition began in 1184 with a Papal Bull decreed by Pope Lucius III. It was created to do away with a growing Catharist movement in southern France which was viewed as heretical and a threat to the church. The Spanish Inquisition did not exist until 1478. The Spanish was vastly different than the Roman Inquisition. For example, the Roman Inquisition answered to and was financed by the church. Whereas the Spanish Inquisition answered to the Spanish monarchy. There are no records showing they were financed from the Royal Treasury. Instead, they got a good portion of the wealth they confiscated from the accused heretics. They were directed by the monarchy to find Jews that had claimed they were converted Catholics but were secretly practicing Judaism. I should add they did the same to the Moors.

In early Christianity, many converts continued to practice some Mosaic practices such as circumcision and abstinence of certain foods, etc.... The apostle Paul met with the apostle Peter to discuss the matter. It was determined that gentiles did not have to be circumcised and if they had a clear conscious, could eat anything as long as it was not sacrificed to idols. The argument was that Jesus brought in a new covenant. The Apostle Peter agreed if Jewish Christians want to continue practicing Mosaic rules from the old covenant, they should continue but not insist on gentile Christians to follow suite. As far as what to eat, **Matthew 15:11** says *"Not that which goeth into the mouth defileth a man: but that which cometh out of the mouth, this defileth a man."* This is further made clear in **I Cor 6:12** *"all things are permissible but not all things are profitable.* (Being aware the following comment is off subject; I am compelled to make it nevertheless.) I have heard many Christians state that smoking cigarettes is a sin and defiles the body which is the temple of the Holy Spirit. However, having the freedom this last verse gives and still practice the discipline of abstinence demonstrates having wisdom and the fruit of temperance, so not doing so in all likelihood will prevent shortening your years. So then asking for wisdom and then walking in it is a freedom in Christ that is to be celebrated.

The Monarch of Spain was very suspicious of Jewish converts. It had been reported that many were still honoring and practicing Mosaic law. I agree with Paul and do not think it is necessary but not harmful either. Let us not forget Jesus honored Mosaic Law. He just disputed the man-made doctrines that the church leaders invented to be self-righteous and claimed would earn their salvation. Until the death of Christ, they were under the old covenant. The Jewish converts were preaching that Jesus was the Messiah so it seems they should have been left alone. The bible states in **Luke 10:49-50** *And John answered and said, "Master, we saw one casting out devils in thy name and forbad him because he followeth not us" and Jesus said unto him "Forbid him not: for he that is not against us is for us"*. Rome had allowed people of all faiths to live in Rome without causing the Catholic church to crumble or political rule to crash. So, what was the formation of the Spanish Inquisition really all about?

The point being, I cannot see how you can be a Christian and torture and burn people alive because a convert wants to keep the Mosaic Law that Jesus himself practiced. But it seems that the early church wanted to control the thoughts of men and have absolute power. In the first five years after the Spanish Inquisition had started, it is estimated that 50,000 people were put to death.

There are some verses in the Bible that suggest reincarnation is possible and the prophet Elijah came back as John the Baptist. In the early church, reincarnation was widely believed until the church pronounced it as heretical. They did that, I think, because it would be harder to control people and to sell them absolution if they thought they could reincarnate. With reincarnation, a person could disagree with the church and not necessarily go to hell. You could just reincarnate. The early church certainly did not want that thought floating around. The Church did not call it selling absolution. It was just paying a penance after you repent. I suppose if you were wealthy, you could afford to do a lot more sinning than a poor man and still go to Heaven. If reincarnation can happen, I am sure that Hitler in a previous life was a Spanish Inquisitor.

After Ferdinand and Isabelle were married, Spain became unified. It was determined that Jews were a threat to the unification of a Catholic Spain. To help solve the problem the Crown requested and obtained a Papal Bull from Pope Sixtus IV to establish a Spanish Inquisition. This Inquisition was not controlled by Rome but by the Royal Crown in Spain. Since money was not paid out of The Royal Treasury it appears they financed themselves. Money that was confiscated was sent to the Royal Crown, and the Inquisition, also, each diocesan cathedral in Spain paid funds to the inquisition, and a reward was paid to whoever made an accusation against someone. It seems reasonable to assume confiscation was a major financing tool of the inquisition. I should mention trials were held in secret and the names of accusers were kept a secret. Under those circumstances, I am sure there was no shortage of accusers. Plus, if someone knew something that could be an accusation and did not report it to the Inquisition, they could be charged with a crime for not reporting. The Inquisition was above everyone except the Royal Crown. They even put a Catholic bishop on trial.

So, because of the persecution, many Jews that were baptized and became Catholic Jews had been living in Spain for several centuries and developed a well-to-do and a wealthy merchant class. Many were well-educated with jobs in government and elsewhere. There was much jealousy of the Jews because of how well they were doing financially. Many converted Jews had intermarried and some of the very wealthy converts had married members of the royal family.

However, the "converted Jews" were viewed suspiciously and were thought to be illegitimate converts. The Inquisition was supposed to be able to find those falsely claiming the conversion.

In 1492 Inquisitor General de Torvemada had the Catholic monarch to expel all Jews who refused to convert. An estimated of 160,000 were expelled with not a lot of time to leave Spain. I should mention that Islamic Moors were driven out as well. With that many people leaving, I would guess there to have been a huge sale on their property at a fraction of value. I would say many people took advantage of that sale.

Jewish converts had been keeping some of their Jewish laws since the beginning. Jewish converts were living in Rome without them destroying the church. Due to the lack of biblical knowledge and church leaders speaking out regarding the deep roots Christianity has in Judaism, the mistrust was not lowered any. It would not be surprising to find out that most Spaniards at this time in history didn't even know Jesus to be Jewish. When the Christian bible was initially constructed, leaving the Old Testament out had been considered because of the emphasis on Judaism and the Jewish people. There were some that wanted to ignore that fact. If the masses had Bibles and they wanted to read and study, they may have thought differently.

The leading Jewish religious leaders developed a strong hate for Jesus as he would correct them publicly on their doctrines. On one occasion he cited the scripture in **Matthew 15:9** *"But in vain they worship me. Teaching for doctrine the commandments of man".* Other verses in the bible explain why Jewish religious leaders disliked Jesus. **Matthew 15:7-8** *"Ye hypocrites, well did Esaias prophesy of you. Saying 'This people draweth nigh unto me with their mouth and honoureth me with their lips: but their heart is far from me".*

Jesus publicly called the rabbis hypocrites that loved the prestige and put needless burdens on men. Consequently, the Rabbis plotted to have Jesus killed but Jesus was extremely popular. They decided to secretly take him into custody at night on a charge of heresy. Judea was under the control of the Roman Empire and the death penalty could only be accomplished with Roman consent. After convicting Jesus, they delivered him to Pontius Pilate who Rome had appointed as the Prefect of Judea. Pilate knew the accusers were acting out of jealousy. **Matthew 27:18** *"For he knew that for envy they had delivered him."*

At the insistence of the mob being instigated by the leading rabbis and elders, Pontius Pilate sentenced him to be crucified and Roman soldiers took him to be crucified. After announcing the death penalty Pilate said **Matthew 27:24** *"When Pilate saw that he could prevail nothing, but that rather a tumult was made. He* *took water, and washed his hands before the multitude, saying, I am innocent of the blood of this just person: see ye to it".*

Rabbis had studied the Old Testament scriptures and knew about the prophecies of a coming Messiah. To them Jesus did not meet their expectations. They no doubt, expected someone that agreed with their doctrines and would also recruit them to be apostles. So, who bears the blame for killing Jesus? Was it Rome? Was it Rome's designated ruler in Jerusalem? Was it the Jews? Or was it the Jewish religious leaders? In 380 AD the Roman Empire made Christianity the official state religion which started the Roman Catholic Church. It is understandable why Rome was never blamed for the death of Christ. However, after a few centuries, you would think that the Catholic leadership would mention the possibilities to quench the anti-Semitism in the world. It could be debated who is the most at fault all day long. We should remember what Jesus said on the cross in **Luke 23:34** *"Father, forgive them, for they do not know what they are doing"*. The church could have explained that Jesus wanted whoever to be forgiven so as Christians we should try to follow his example. There were many Jews and Muslims that had gone to the Spanish colonies, so the Inquisition decided to go there and do their corruption and evil work. Possibly the number of targets in Spain were getting smaller.

Since my goal is to prove with scripture that these acts of atrocities cannot be blamed on Christianity, I am going to focus on that goal. If a person wants more detail on these atrocities, I suggest a book titled *"Inquisition: The Reign of Fear"* by Toby Green. He gives many examples of atrocities, cruelties, and corruption. The Inquisition is a good example of what was being said in Ephesians 6:12 *"For we do not wrestle against flesh and blood, but against principalities, against powers, against the rulers of the darkness of this world, against spiritual wickedness in high places."*

I remember an instance in my past where a drunk driver killed the child of an Amish family. The family said they had forgiven the man and wanted charges dropped. I truly don't think I could be that forgiving but I admired their faith. Jesus forgave the people that were killing him while he was dying *on the cross. I can say with any conviction that Jesus would not* condone what the Inquisition was doing in his name. If there were evil people pretending to be Christians, it seems the Inquisitors were the truly guilty ones. We are warned in the Bible that such evil would be in the world in high places to deceive because their God is the love of money and power. I think most people want to do right but get deceived. This is why we must, as Christians read the Bible and fact-check our spiritual and political leaders.

On March 11, 1649, a large procession left the Holy Office of the Inquisition in Mexico City. The procession weaved its way through the city to announce the coming of a trial of faith in a month. It would take a month to set up everything for the event which was supposed to be an earthly representation of the heavenly judgment. It was a beautiful event with music and fine decorations to represent a heavenly place. The procession was led by musicians and were followed by ministers of the Holy Office of the Inquisition and followed by many of the nobility and the rear was brought up by Don Juan Alguire de Soaznava, the chief warden of the Inquisition of Mexico. An exceptionally large stage was built around eight marbled columns. There were paintings on and around the stage. A pyramid was built and decorated with the shield of the faith. It was very grand in appearance. It was estimated that about 20,000 people attended the event to watch the beating and burning of live humans. Reading about it reminded me of how Christians were fed to lions in their arenas for entertainment. The mass slaughter of Christians started with Emperor Nero AD 64 and went on and off for several centuries. Emperor Trajan AD 98-117 held four months straight a public ceremony where Christians were fed to lions. It was estimated that 11,000 Christians were killed. Non-Christians did this. Yet, centuries later similar cruelties are being done by people claiming to be Christians. The Bible verses mentioned in chapter 1 that instructed on how to convert people to Christianity in a peaceful manner as Jesus taught. I know that priests and monks could read, and I am sure they had read those verses. Why did they not protest the Inquisition trails?

On the day of the event, church bells rang. Fifteen people were sentenced to death for secretly practicing Judaism. All but one declared they were baptized Catholics. One of the fifteen declared he was guilty. For declaring he was guilty he was burned alive. The fourteen who declared they were innocent would be strangled to death and then burned. It seems to have no logic. Only a resolute man or woman who wants to make a point would declare they are guilty.

The native Indians were not targeted by the Inquisition. The priests oversaw converting them and agriculture and ore mining needed them for cheap labor. Many Indians fled and hid in isolated jungles or mountains. I figure there was no profit in going after poor native Indians since everything they owned had already been stolen. I should mention at this trial of faith many people who were there who had not been found guilty of a death sentence were tried and given a penance such as lashings, imprisonment, etc... most always confiscation of family goods was a penance they had to pay. What my grandmother would have said about the beauty and grandeur of the trial of faith, "You can't make a silk purse out of a sow's ear." That is indeed an old saying going back to the 15th century. For those that have not heard that old saying, it means you cannot make something ugly into something beautiful. It was first found written in English by Alexander Barclay Eclogues (1472-1552). He was a Scottish clergyman and poet. It is believed he is the first person to write the proverb in English.

CHAPTER III

THE WITCH TRIALS

Exodus 22:18 Thou shall not suffer a witch to live.

The witch trials are another example of atrocities that many people blame on Christianity. I am going to address that topic, but first I want to go back to the Old Testament to see what is said on the subject and try to put it into context. God had made a covenant promise to Abraham that the land of Canaan would be given to him and his seed to inhabit as a possession. However, it was many centuries later before the Israelites went there to possess the land. Which was sometimes described as a land "flowing with milk and honey".

God told the people in **Deuteronomy 18: 10-12** *"Thereshall not be found among you any one that maketh his son or daughter to pass through the fire, or that useth divination, or an observer of times, or an enchanter, or a witch or a charmer, or a consulter with familiar spirits, or a wizard, or a necromancer for all that do these things are* *an abomination unto the Lord: and because of these abominations the Lord thy God doth drive them out from before thee".*

God had previously told the people in **Deuteronomy 9:6,** *"Understand, therefore, that the Lord thy God giveth thee not this good land to possess it for thy righteousness; for thou art a stiff-necked people"* God was reminding them of their previous rebellions against Moses who was giving them God's instructions. So, God told the people it was not for their righteousness; He was giving them the land so they would be humble. God expected his people to think of him as their source and they did not need magic or other gods for things like fertility.

Canaan had many gods, but Baal was considered the king of all the gods. Baal was the fertility god and Canaan was very productive agriculturally. The people wanted to appease Baal in hopes of abundant crops. The rituals included anything that might aid fertility, not excluding sex rituals. The temples hosted male and female prostitution, bestiality, and child sacrifice by fire. The child sacrifice was typically a son or a daughter. God chose to drive these people out before his chosen people occupied the land. Plus, he wanted none of those people to stay because they could be a snare or temptation to his chosen people. God explained to the people they did not need soothsayers, witches, sorcery, etc. because he will send prophets to guide them. In the year 2021, there are still people that will tell your fortune for a fee. Other people claim for a fee they will help you communicate with the spirits of loved ones that have passed away. I suspect, it is used today to separate gullible people from their money. The practices were just more used and believed than in modern times. The commercials for fortune-telling usually run late at night. I have known a few people that have called those fortune tellers "psychics".

What is a witch according to the Old Testament? The word written in Hebrew was "Mekhashepha" of which no one knows the exact meaning in the Old Testament. We only have various interpretations made many centuries later. Merrill F Unger, a Biblical scholar and theologian interpreted a witch as one who practices magic by using occult formulas, incantations, and mystic mutterings. Kenneth Kitchen, a bible scholar at the University of Liverpool translates the root as "to cut". Suggesting it could be like an herbalist. That interpretation comes close to Septuagint a translation from Hebrew to Greek around the third century. Since it was translated by Jewish scholars in Egypt and they also knew Greek, it is thought they might be the best source but there is no certainty many scholars disagree. Since Baal was considered the God of fertility, perhaps witches provided potions to help the worshipper be more fertile at home, their orgies, and religious ceremonies. Maybe this could be where the term Love Potion started as an ancient form of Viagra.

I am not qualified to say that is what the Bible was referring to when it was written. What I am saying is if the root of the word meant "to cut" and no one really knows what is the correct translation, who knows? In 382 AD the Old Testament was translated into Latin which defined it as a witch, and it appears as years went by it was redefined as someone with who Satan had made a pact.

Exodus 22:18 *"Thou shalt not suffer a witch to live"* is the verse that was used to justify executing people, mostly women. I think translators should have known that they did not know the exact meaning of the Hebrew word since it was written thousands of years earlier. Even Jewish scholars did not know for sure the exact meaning. As I will point out with the help of the bible, those executions were not committed by the Christianity teachings of Jesus or his Apostles.

Basically, God promised the Hebrews that if they followed his commandments and laws, he would bless them. If they did not follow his laws, he would curse them, and sometimes the land itself. He always promised that eventually, he would restore them after they repented and went back to Mosaic law. Over the centuries the Hebrews did backslide on many occasions and started worshipping other gods and practicing soothsaying, witchcraft, and other occult practices. Even in the New Testament, occult practices were around.

Acts 19:18-19 *"and many that believed came, and confessed, and showed their deeds and many of them also that used curious arts brought their books together and burned them before all men: and they counted the price of them and found it fifty thousand pieces of silver."*

Considering the value, I would think that the occult practice then was much like today, being lovers of money. However, at the point of this book burning they repented and could then join Christianity. They were not put to death under Mosaic law. Instead, they were forgiven as Jesus had taught. Some of them may have believed in their magic rituals. I think many were in it for the money as they charged fees for their services just like they do in modern times. There is nothing new under the sun when it comes to human nature and money.

Let us now discuss the practice of witchcraft and how the early churches treated the subject. A book called *"The Witch"* by Ronald Hutton does a superb job in studying the subject. Much of the book was based on a global archaeological study of societies throughout history. Magic, sorcery and practicing witches have been found to be in all societies in some form or another. Many found their way into the local churches leaving their grave, negative and deadly spiritual imprint.... and do still to this day.

Sorcery was practiced nearly universally by those who had learned its magic. It was and still is a craft taught today. Ceremonial sorcery was usually performed for a fee and could be used for good or evil. Whereas witches work for the dark side because they are born inherently evil.

In 1692, an outbreak of witchcraft took place in Massachusetts which was led by Protestants. Stacy Schiff, author of *"THE WITCH: Salem 1692"* did excellent research on the Salem witch trials. He tells of a clergyman who had two children in his home who were given to convulsions and continual hysterical behavior. One was a niece and the other his daughter. He did, however, have other children that were normal. In modern times this would most likely be diagnosed as neurological or an inherited disorder. Over time, the two children did not recover so it was thought they were bewitched and the hunt for the witch(es) that were responsible began. Many churches, understanding the spirit realm, practice the deliverance of demonic spirits today.

Early Europeans thought that witches mostly hurt people in the community including the aristocrats or even the king. Eventually, in time it was believed that witches were not only evil but had a pact with Satan. I suggest the book mentioned above for more details on this. It appears that the pact with Satan was a Christian add-on to the local pagan thoughts about witches. At around the same time, ceremonial magic was getting complimentary reviews. The sorcerer was described as a priest dedicated to the worship of the one true God and had learned how to influence or predict the future for good. And, also, for a fee. Regardless, a Church campaign against ceremonial magic had been tried in order to stop those events. A handbook called "The Sworn Book of Herodias" was written in response to the Church campaign. According to the book *"The Witch"* the introduction audaciously asserted that the Pope and his Cardinals were themselves possessed by demons and that it was the magicians who served the cause of truth, under the inspiration of the Christian God, were exemplars of piety and offered a sure means of salvation." I do not think the Pope and his Cardinals were demon-possessed. In my opinion, the Catholic Church was already losing much control in Europe because of the Protestant movement, and they viewed these ceremonies as a pending threat that would further erode Catholic religious authority. Evidently, the campaign did not work since magic ceremonies continued in most of Europe that had a strong Protestant population. I am sure that most people have heard about Merlin the Wizard who supposedly helped England's, King Arthur. The myth of Merlin shows how sorcery was not considered totally evil by many people. It appears the Catholic church was more interested in eradicating Jewish and Muslim heretics than witches. There was certainly more profit in trying heretics than witches.

It seems to me that if you needed an evil reason for the children's behavior, demon possession would be a better choice. It would make more biblical sense. In the New Testament, there are many scriptures about demons. Jesus himself spoke of casting out demons. His apostles did the same. In one instance, the apostles were unable to cast out a demon, so they asked Jesus about the matter. Jesus replied, **Matthew 17:20** *"However this kind goeth not out but by prayer and fasting"*. Exorcism was more of a Catholic practice. Whereas Salem, Massachusetts was a Protestant community, and witches were blamed for the behavior of the clergyman's two children.

It is very apparent the bible does not give a clear picture of what a witch did in ancient Israel. The notion that they flew at night on sticks or brooms, killed and ate the organs of children at nighttime satanic gatherings was a carry-over from the folklore of pagan religions. These folklores existed in the European region prior to their conversion to Christianity. Thoughts that had become incorporated into the beliefs of many Christians, even though, there are no bible verses to support such thoughts. It is amazing that many priests, pastors, and scholars who spent much of their lives studying scripture would endorse the torture and execution of people as witches.

Especially, when you see how confessions and accusations were obtained. The lesson to be learned from this is that even laypeople need to read the scriptures and look for verses that support their spiritual leaders' direction. To protect the truth from being distorted by self-righteous people who add to the scriptures. The Pharisees and Sadducees were doing just this when Jesus called them out for it.

Matthew15:9 *"But they do worship me, teaching for doctrines the commandments of men".* Eventually, the two children told a story about how they were taken at night by flying witches. They also identified the witches, so the hunt and executions commenced. A common form of torture was to hang them upside down till their noses bled. After two to four days without sleep, cognitive impairments and even hallucinations can occur. I am sure that it would be hard to sleep under these conditions. These people were kept like this for weeks or months. If they confessed to being a witch and name other witches with stories, they could get better treatment. No more hanging upside down, the shackles are removed, a little more sleep, etc. Arrest and convictions under these circumstances snowballed. Children were accusing parents and siblings. Even young children were arrested and convicted. Wives accused husbands, and even clergymen were accused. No one was safe regardless of your social position. Individual rights under common law did not apply to witch trials. These people were not even given the protections the bible gave them or the protection of common law.

2 Corinthians 13:1 *"This is the third time I am coming to you. In the mouth of two or three witnesses shall every word be established."* What happened in Massachusetts? Many of the judges had gone to Harvard. These people had studied scripture. They had to see there was no clear definition of a witch in the Bible. I am sure they had read the New Testament verses already discussed that people who were practicing ceremonial magic had repented and burned their magic text and were welcomed in the Christian church. These scholars, also, had to know that much of the thoughts on witches were add-ons from the early pagan myths from cultures that Christianity had converted, mostly Europe. That is another reason I find the trials and executions amazing. These men must have been worried about the opinions of their peers to go along with stories of night-flying witches going to satanic worship services. They may have been afraid of being accused themselves. Years after the trials, some people did come forward and confessed, they falsely accused and made-up stories. But before judging them harshly, we should remember the torture they were put through. There is nothing in the bible especially in the New Testament that can be used to justify the witch trials. As usual, the trials were justified by the doctrine and commandments of men, and I am certain there were those that knew this but did not speak up about the matter. So, these trials were not the works of Christianity and bible beliefs. Furthermore, Satan was not using a coven of witches to do evil. Satan had some self-righteous witch trial judges to do evil. He did not need witches.

CHAPTER IV

THE CRUSADES

Romans 12:18 "if it be possible, as much as lieth in you, live peaceable with all men".

In 1095 CE, the Byzantine Emperor Alexios Komnenos sent Ambassadors to Pope Urban II to ask for help against the Persian Muslims. The Ambassadors claimed that the Muslims had taken control of Christian lands and killed or captured many Christians in the process. Captives were typically sold into a lifetime of slavery. The women that were young or virgins were usually sold as sex slaves. The Ambassadors went on to say these things were happening in Churches that were inside and outside the Byzantine Empire. even in Jerusalem. Therefore, The Emperor was asking the Pope to help him regain his empire and save Jerusalem.

Constantinople was a grand and heavily fortified city with access to the Mediterranean Sea for sea trade, as well, as a focal point for land travel between Europe and the east such as, India and China. It was formerly known as the Eastern Roman Empire after the Roman Empire had split into a western and eastern empire. The grandeur of Constantinople became as magnificent as Rome. The two empires had different leaders with the west becoming the Byzantine Empire. Emperor Komnenos had watched his empire being slowly taken over by the Persian Muslims. Constantinople was not in immediate danger, but the emperor knew it was only a matter of time before the Muslim warriors would be at the walls and that was the main reason, he asked the Pope to build an army to fight the Muslims to keep his existing power and regain lost territory.

The pope accepted the challenge and saw this as a way to unite European Catholics. At that time, the church and the Emperor of Rome were not on good terms. The church had excommunicated the Roman Emperor several times. In retaliation, the emperor had appointed several anti-popes who were not recognized by the rest of Europe or even Italy. Years earlier the church had asked the Germans for help, and they came, and, in the process, Germans ransacked Rome and burned half of the city. Germany was Roman Catholic and supported the Papacy and I suspect the Roman Emperor did not want the Germans to revisit Rome, so he did not try to replace and install a pope of his choice.

The pope was having large outside events in Europe to recruit volunteers to help liberate Jerusalem. The march to Jerusalem started at Constantine liberating cities in the Byzantine Empire from Muslim oppression. I would like to mention that many of the Christian churches in the west that would be liberated were Greek Orthodox Christian churches as well as Roman Catholic churches.

The pope knew that he needed knights and princes to join so he appealed to such men throughout Europe. These were the men who had experience in war and leading men into battle. The voyage was going to be expensive and most of these men had the financial means to recruit other men of war and finance the task. The Pope wanted the volunteers to pay their own way. Many people rich and poor took out mortgages to provide for the journey. These men were promised remission of their sins, their families would be protected by the church from creditors, and any interest that would have been charged. Plus, it was understood that the Crusaders could plunder a city after it is conquered. I am sure that the remission of sins and the pride of belonging to the army of the Holy Church was a great motivator. The knowledge that they could plunder and take everything of value from the conquered territory with the church's permission was also a motivator. I suspect, for some the right to plunder may have been the main motivator. Amongst the Knights and princes, there was the hope that land would be given, and they would be made Lords. After all, many of the princes that took part in the crusades were not the first born sons in their families and, therefore could not inherit the bulk of the land that belonged to their father since that went to the first born by tradition. For these other sons, the best way to acquire great wealth and power was with the sword. For the second and third sons that managed to stay alive through the many battles that took place during the march to Jerusalem, some of them got land and Lordships granted to them.

The pope was putting an army led by Christian warriors with experience in battle and the development of a chain of command. The princes could also raise the money needed to finance the campaign. At the same time, he was recruiting men from all walks of life. As already mentioned, mortgaging their property was the only way they could make such a trip. This war would be by a multi-national group of men led by the aristocratic princes from across Europe. While the Pope was busy building the church's holy army, another man named Peter the Hermit, who was thought of as a religious recluse, decided to get involved. He was a well-traveled man who was up in years, He was described as charismatic and preached to the people why they needed to help liberate and save the Christians from the Muslim pagans. He indeed raised a large following but unlike the pope's armies, they were made up of mostly commoners such as farmers, shop workers, etc... His army had few men with war or leadership experience or a good chain of command. I believe the events that took place will validate my opinion. As the reader will see Peter the Hermit was, also, very anti-Semitic.

The pope and his princes which I will refer to as generals had set up a timeline where they would travel across Europe to Constantinople in several large groups.Peter the Hermit did not want to wait so his holy army took off much earlier.On their way, they went through Hungary where there was a large Jewish settlement. Keep in mind the church had declared that charging interest on loans was not Christian and not allowed. Therefore, loaning money with interest became a Jewish monopoly creating many wealthy Jewish money changers. Well, Peter the Hermit preached that Jews were also enemies of Christ and should be eliminated. His followers went on to murder, rape, and plunder the Jews for everything they could find. It was recorded they even killed the Jews that claimed they had converted to Christianity. It was reported that a local priest had tried to hide about six hundred Jews, but the crusaders found them and killed them. Mothers had killed their own children and themselves to keep from being taken alive and tortured. After that happened Hungary, for a while, closed its borders to traveling Crusaders. The official response from the church condemned what happened. The church said Jews are to be converted not murdered. I found nothing where the pope instructed Peter the Hermit to turn around and go back to his home.

Peter the Hermit got to Constantinople months before the other generals and their armies. The news of what he did in Hungary had reached the emperor's ears. He welcomed the arriving army and thanked them for their help, but only a few, including Peter the Hermit, could enter the city. The army itself was told to camp outside the city's walls. The Imperial Princess Anna Komnene kept a journal throughout her life, and she thought Peter the Hermit and his army were a bunch of smelly vulgar vagabonds. Peter the Hermit did not want to wait for the other generals to arrive, so his army marched to the nearest Muslim-held city. They were no match against the experienced Muslim warriors. The Crusaders were decimated rather quickly and easily. Peter the Hermit managed to escape and return to Constantinople. I found no information on others that might have escaped but I am sure there must have been others. I only assume that because of the expense of the trip anyone that might have escaped most likely joined another general. Peter the Hermit was out of the crusading business.

The other generals arrived at Constantinople a group at a time. The emperor promised protection to any pilgrims passing through his area. The generals took a vow to return the cities that had been a part of his empire back to him after they conquered and plundered the city of everything of value.There were many cities to be taken before reaching Jerusalem and several had been part of the Byzantine empire. Because they needed to take over the Muslim-controlled cities before going to Jerusalem, it was not reached quickly.

I will not spend much time going through each battle. Instead, I will only cover their most difficult battle which appeared to be Antioch. Something I found most interesting is that they had Christians and Jews living in Antioch. They could live, work, and practice their own religious faith there if they paid a hefty tax for the privilege. These people could have moved elsewhere but chose to live in Antioch under Muslim control. From what I had read this was the Muslim practice in the areas they had conquered. I suspect, these Christians would have preferred to have their communities under Christian control. The fact that they chose to live there and pay a hefty tax leads me to believe they were doing well financially and were not being harassed or tortured by the Muslims. Those reports from the ambassadors that were sent from the emperor to the pope requesting help appear to have been exaggerated. I think history shows that the emperor was mostly worried about his power and wealth and not Jerusalem.

I would also mention that the Christian men in Antioch were expelled from the city, but the women and children remained in the city. The Muslims did that because they were afraid that the men would cause a resurrection within the walls. Antioch was well supplied with water and food.

While the Crusaders were not a problem, hunger and thirst posed as a threat, especially through the winter. The attack might have been abandoned, except a general named Bohemond was able to get someone on the inside of the city to turn traitor for a high reward. The traitor managed to get the Crusaders access into the city.Bohemond started the crusade with only a few thousand men, but he took credit for taking the city. After taking the city the Crusaders plundered and killed the inhabitants, even the Jews. Bohemond and his troops decided to stay in Antioch where Bohemond decided to take control and rule the new Christian colony. He reneged on his vow to return the city back to the emperor. Bohemond was an aristocrat, and this is exactly what he wanted. He decided to let the other Crusaders liberate the other cities including Jerusalem which was the main rallying point when it all started. Bohemond's reason for not honoring his oath to the emperor was that the emperor had not sent his own troops to help at Antioch when the Crusaders were going to have to withdraw from the siege if not for the betrayal from within the walls as already mentioned. Bohemond raised his own flag over the city and decided to stay and become the governor of the newly established Christian colony. This siege ended in June 1098. The crusaders that did not stay in Antioch marched on to Jerusalem. While in route to Jerusalem they conquered many more Islamic-controlled cities.

Jerusalem was governed by Governor Iftikhar Al-Sawda. He only had about 1,000 soldiers but he felt certain that Fatima in Egypt was going to send him help. Jerusalem was well fortified with its own water supply. All water wells near Jerusalem had been destroyed to make it difficult for the crusaders. These Crusaders consisted of about 15,000 men which is about a third of what they had when they started their march. The governor understood the Crusaders were very fatigued and many were sick. Because of all these conditions, the governor was not overly concerned. I am sure that changed as time went by and he never got reinforcements from Egypt, and on July 15, 1099, Jerusalem fell. The governor of Jerusalem made a deal to save himself and the remaining soldiers, so they were escorted to the nearest Muslim-controlled city. There were thousands of Muslims and Jewish citizens left in the city to be plundered and murdered by the Crusaders. They were beheaded and had limbs amputated. Piles of heads and limbs were outside city walls. Many committed suicide to escape being tortured. Jews hid in their synagogue to escape but the synagogue was set on fire with them inside. When the Jews were killed in Hungary, the pope said the Jews were not to be killed but rather they should be converted. The mob was out of control with no effective leadership. The mob was more interested in plundering the Jews than converting them to Christianity.

Jerusalem remained in Christian control until 1187 CE when it was retaken by Saladin the sultan of Egypt and Syria. What took so long is that the Islamic world was divided between several factions with each faction wanting control of more territory. There were the Sunnis in the middle east and, also, the sultan in Baghdad which controlled most of Persia then there were several lesser warlords.Saladin had even signed peace agreements with some of the Christian colonies including Jerusalem. He figured they would function as a buffer between Egypt and Persia. The peace treaties would also let him use his resources to battle his Islamic enemies. Even as it is today, there was disagreement over who should be the top religious leader. Saladin wished to establish his authority as a top religious leader before retaking Jerusalem. When the 10-year peace treaty with Jerusalem expired, he was ready to war against Jerusalem and retook it in 1187 CE.

I would like to mention that even before the crusades started, Islam leaders had expanded throughout Persia, Assyria, the Middle East, Israel, Egypt, and Northern Africa, Mediterranean Islands such as Sicily, Portugal, and parts of Spain. If you were a Christian or Jewish, you would be allowed to continue to live and work in the territory if you paid a hefty tax to the new leader. If you were not Christian or Jewish (a man with a book as Muslims referred to them) it would be wise to become Muslim if you wanted to live. This expansion was led by many different

Sultans and warlords because the Islamic world was not united under one leader. Jerusalem Crusaders had asked the pope for reinforcements. He did rally again for Crusaders, however, he requested that they go to Spain and Portugal to help expel the Muslim invaders and reestablish the countries as Christian dominated nations. I need to point this out because so far, my writings make it sound like the Muslims were victims. The various sultans and warlords were very ruthless while expanding their territory to obtain more riches and power. I do commend them on letting Christians and Jews continue practicing their faith, working, and residing in their homes as long as they paid a hefty tax. I am not sure if they did this for humane reasons or the tax was a nice source of revenue. It seems power and gold can corrupt people of all religions.

The Crusaders that went to Spain and Portugal make sense because they were helping countries fight against invading armies. The Muslims were conquering occupiers. The march on Jerusalem is a different matter. It seems the Byzantine Emperor wanted to protect Constantinople from Muslim invasion and hopefully regain some of his former empires in Persia. Arabs always inhabited Persia and Assyria. So, from the Arabs point of view, the Christians were invaders. It also appears the emperor made up lies about how the Muslims were treating Christians. He told those lies to stir up the hearts of Christians to get their help. However, long before this happened Muslim Sultans and Warlords had been invading Christian nations in Europe and the Mediterranean. Since they allowed Christians and Jews to continue living in the areas they conquered, the invasions must not have been to convert the population to Islam. The Muslim conquerors were mostly after power and loot. I saved this chapter for the last chapter of Part 1 because it is most difficult to respond with a satisfactory answer. The church as well as other Christians justified the march to Jerusalem on Old Testament writings. God told the Hebrews to go and take Canaan which is the land God had promised to them. God told the Hebrews he was doing this not because they had been so righteous, but the Canaanites were so evil. Also, God wanted them completely driven out of the land so they would not be a snare to the Israelites.

GENESIS 12: 1-3 *"Now the Lord had said unto Abram, Get thee out of thy country, and from thy kindred, and from thy fathers house, unto a land that I will shew thee: 2And I will make of thee a great nation, and I will bless thee, and make thy name great: and thou shalt be a blessing: 3 And I will bless them that bless the, and curse him that curseth thee: and in thee shall all families of the earth be blessed".*

There are many verses in the Bible that clearly state that God was giving that land to the Hebrews. There are many verses that say God will bless those that bless Israel. One would think that if the Crusaders wanted to be in line with scripture, they would be liberating Jerusalem to turn control over to the Hebrews. The Bible states many times that land was given to Abraham and his seed for possession. So, it would be much more Christian to conquer Jerusalem and turn it over to Hebrews than to loot the city and murder the Jews inhabiting the city. The pope was very worried about Rome being invaded by Muslims they were advancing in Europe and the

Mediterranean. It was apparent the Muslims did not care if you keep your religion. They just wanted the power and wealth of the lands they invaded. The blame for the crusades can be blamed on many things including the lust for power and wealth by the Muslim sultans and warlords. The pope should have thought back when Christians were being persecuted. During that time, Christianity grew, and eventually, it became the state religion. The early Christians endured the persecution with love, not with a sword. Those people demonstrated the Christian way to overcome fear. As always it was the desire for money and power that caused the crusades.

CONCLUSION

PART ONE

Christianity is and has always been used by powerful people to disguise their personal lust for riches, power, and prestige. These people have been very deceptive, causing many people to believe they are godly men. They do this by gaining trust, teaching pleasant things and mislead in doctrinal truths. The truths of the scriptures are hidden from them, so they won't be found out to be the false teachers they are.

Matthew 7:15 *"Beware of false prophets, which come to you in sheep's clothing but inwardly they are ravenous wolves".*

Jesus told the religious leaders they were enforcing doctrines of men as if the doctrines were commandments. While doing this, they themselves were not following a God given commandment. In many cases, ignorance of scripture or lack of being a Christian could be blamed for a person's action. Ignorance is not new.

Paul the Apostle said about himself in **1Timothy 1:13** *"Was before a blasphemer, and a persecutor, and injurious: but I obtained* *mercy because I did it ignorantly in unbelief."* This, however, is not the case for a false teacher, pastor or prophet.

Prior to having the spirit of Jesus pay him a visit, the Christians feared Paul. Paul thought it was his duty to annihilate Christians. As I have previously said, the best way to avoid acting out of ignorance is to not assume your leaders are correct and use the Bible to validate what is being taught.

II Timothy 2:15 *"Study to show yourself approved unto God, a workman needs not to be ashamed, rightly dividing the word of truth".*

It helps me to also listen to various clergy speakers because sometimes their lectures can open a window of insight that can be beneficial to my understanding. No matter how much I learn, I can always learn more. When it comes to God, I suspect there is not a person that will know it all. Our goal as Christians is to follow the teachings and examples of Jesus and his apostles. Achieving this goal of course is easier said than done and is a never-ending process. It is clearly stated that we are all sinners and struggle against the lust of the flesh. This is one of the reasons Jesus tells us to come into his rest that his burden is light. Regardless of how difficult it may be, we are supposed to strive for that goal. There are millions of people throughout history and today that have done and do just that. Over seventy-seven million people in the U.S.A. alone, contribute their time and money to charity. Christian churches and individuals donate resources around the world helping the sick and poor.

I have however, met people that will walk into a church looking for some action they think is not a Christian act and immediately condemn everyone in the church. Such a person does not understand we are all sinners. The only difference between the Christian sinner and non-Christian sinner is the Christian knows they are a sinner. Prior to being Executed Jesus said **John:16** *"And I will pray for the Father, and he shall give you another Comforter, that he may abide with you forever".* This comforter which he sends is better known as the Holy Spirit which is to help guide us to do things that would be pleasing to God. I think of it as a spiritual compass.

My writing is not anti-Catholic. Throughout history millions of Catholics have tried to live lives based on the biblical doctrines of Christianity. Mother Teresa is a good example. The same can be said of Protestants. The doctrines and examples taught by Jesus and his apostles are not what causes problems. I believe problems start with individuals deciding to start and control their own religion.

I have written Part 1 to stand by itself. I realize it does not meet my second objective stated in the introduction. The following chapters will address that goal. At 69 years old I know that tomorrow is not promised to anyone. Consequently, I thought I should write part 1 so that it could stand alone. If you are reading this and there are no other parts. Most likely, I am in paradise looking up loved ones and old friends.

PART TWO

CHAPTER V

HINDUISM- The soil Buddhism sprang from

ROMANS 2:14-15 NLT *"Even Gentiles, who do not have Gods written law, show that they know his law when they instinctively obey it, even without having heard it. They demonstrate that God s law is written in their hearts, for their own conscience and thoughts either accuse them or tell them they are doing right."*

I started my research into early Hinduism to gain some insight into the life of Siddhartha Gautama, the man who is now known as Buddha. Somewhere between 1800-1500 BC, the Indo-Aryans invaded northern India. They were described as tall light-skinned men from Europe that drove chariots. It started at the Indus River in northern India and spread over time to much of India and Iran. They became the ruling class but obtained assistance from the ruling class that had ruled before the Aryans had arrived. The land was divided into districts with appointed leaders. It was each leader's job to maintain a standing army and appoint priests to perform ceremonies and give spiritual guidance. A book called *Man's Religions* by John B. Noss does a great job of giving more details. For my purpose, I will make it much shorter.

Over decades and centuries, the Aryans spread their influence across India. Four spiritual teachings called the Vedas were taught. The Rig Veda is considered the most sacred. The Vedas describe the rituals for ceremonies as well as daily prayers for separate occasions. Many hymns are often told as a riddle. The Rig Veda mentions the caste system such as priests, the ruling class, producers, and servants. Lower caste was added in other teachings like a caste for drunkards and the untouchables. I am sure if Hillary Clinton were setting up the caste system, there would be the deplorables. There are other lesser teachings than the Vedas. Several different sects of Hinduism were established, usually over a different interpretation of the sacred teachings. I like to think of it as Christianity developing many denominations from the same holy writings. People could choose from many sects. According to *Man's Religion* by John B Noss, "Their only obligation whatever their divergences are to abide by the rules and rituals of their caste and trust that by doing so their next birth will be a happier one." He says next birth in reference to the Hindu belief in reincarnation and the law of Karma. During your life, you do bad things and get bad Karma or do good things and get good Karma. If you get more good Karma than bad, you could reincarnate into a higher caste and eventually work your way up to the upper caste and be able to die and not reincarnate but achieve Nirvana. From what I could tell, Nirvana is some blissful out-of-body existence united with the supreme spirit and not need to reincarnate and return to the physical world. Whereas, if you have some really bad Karma, you could reincarnate and come back as a worm or pig which would make it much longer for you to reach Nirvana.

Hinduism has rules pertaining to their religious ceremonies and rules for each caste, but they also have a moral code to live by to achieve good Karma. Many of the moral codes are similar to those of Christianity and other religions. It appears that there are some morals and values written in the heart no matter what religion you belong as verses already mentioned in Romans 2:14-15 NLT. Having the caste system established in their religious teachings, in my opinion, should make it easier for the ruling caste to control the peasants. Under the law of Karma, if you are a starving peasant, you are getting exactly what you earned in past lives. At the same time, the law of Karma can give hope to the peasant that if he does good things and follows his caste rules, he could acquire enough good Karma to move up the social ladder. Having religious teachings such as these had to make it easier to rule unhappy people. At this time, I would like to mention that Buddhism did not accept the teachings of the Vedas but does accept the law of Karma. The

Vedas prohibited marriage between the different caste. It even had rules against socialization between different caste. I am going to assume that Aryans reproduced with the native ruling class since we have very, if any, tall and light-skinned Indians in modern times. This statement is just an assumption.

I would like to comment on a statement in the book *"Many Many Many Gods of Hinduism: Turning Believers into Nonbelievers"* by Swami Achuthananda. He states, "Hinduism is panentheism in nature." He also writes traditional theism (Christianity) that God is above the world, but not within us, transcendent, but not imminent.

John 16-17 *"And I will pray the Father, and he shall give you another comforter, that: he may abide with you forever; Even the Spirit of truth; whom the world cannot receive, because it seeth him not, neither knoweth him: but ye know him; for he dwelleth with you and shall be in you".* **John 14:20** *"At that day ye shall know that I am in my father, and ye in me, and I in you."*

From scriptures in the bible, it is apparent that Christians have God within them through Jesus Christ. I can easily see how this author could make that mistake or perhaps' I misinterpret him. I read the Bible many times before I realized we have God within us as well as all around us. I am aware that I just got off track here, but I feel compelled to explain that Christians have God within them. It is true that in the Old Testament God was everywhere because nothing can contain him. It mentions many times when the spirit was with someone but not within them. However, 50 days after the death Christ on Pentecost, the Holy Spirit came to dwell in those that accept the gift of eternal life by the forgiveness of our sin through his Grace.

Getting back on track, let me talk about some things regarding Hinduism that's not talked or written about very often and that is human sacrifice. It was made illegal under colonialism, but it continued in secret and still exists today. Bride burning is a good example. Women would be burned alive when their husbands died. At his funeral It was considered the ultimate form of devotion of a good wife. It is safe to assume that Hindu wedding vows did not include "till death do you part." Many women did volunteer because they wanted to earn good Karma. If a woman did not volunteer, it was acceptable for her in-laws to kill her. On June 24, 2003, around 50,000 Hindu monks met in India's northeastern Assam state and vowed to fight the ritual of human sacrifice of children which was being performed secretly in some temples across the country. This was something I had never heard before I began my research. I suspect it is something most Hindus are ashamed of and do not want to publicize. I can only imagine how much more prevalent human sacrifice was at the time the Buddha was born. I only mention it to help give me a glimpse of the culture he lived in.

CHAPTER VI

THE BEGINNING OF BUDDHISM

And Jesus said, John 14:2-3 "In my Father's house are many mansions: if it were not so, I would have told you. I go to prepare a place for you and if I go and prepare a place for you, I will come again, and receive you unto myself: that where I am, there ye may be also."

Siddhartha Gautama was born in Nepal around 500 BCE. He was to become the first Buddha and founder of the initial teachings of Buddhism. He was a prince and by the age of twenty-nine he had a wife and son. Around this time, he noticed how much suffering there was in the world. Suffering such as poverty, hunger, old age, sickness, and death. Because he was young and had lived a sheltered life, he had not noticed the suffering. He also realized that regardless of your caste in life, suffering could not be avoided or eliminated. He gave up his life as a prince and left his wife and son and went on a quest to find a way to eliminate suffering and find inner peace.

He left his home and spent 6 years with monks practicing asceticism, self-control, fasting, and meditation. He realized he was not finding the answers he sought. He felt that what he sought could only be attained with mental discipline. He left the monks and went to a sight in northern India and spent seven days meditating and then realized he was the source of his suffering and the source of the wisdom he sought. He begins his search for enlightenment and started accepting students. He was the first Buddha and Buddhism has grown worldwide over the centuries. Buddha felt you had to be unattached from your senses and that extreme asceticism with lengthy periods of fasting made it more difficult to detach. He believed you should eat early before noon and that starving only made it more difficult to detach yourself from your senses. So extreme fasting he no longer practiced.

In the past, I always thought of the Buddha statue of the fat and smiling monk. It is the most popular symbol of the Buddha in the west, but it is not Siddhartha Gautama. Instead, he was a Zen monk called Budai who lived in China around the 10th century about 1600 years after the original Buddha. He was part of a school of Mahayana Buddhism which was practiced mainly in China, Japan, Korea, and Vietnam. In China being fat was a symbol of prosperity However, in Japan many people considered him to be a glutton. I looked up the eating habits of Zen monks and they ate an early breakfast and a light lunch. That does not sound like gluttony to me. Some Christians think that being overweight is a sin. They base it on scripture that says we are the temple of God's spirit. They read those scriptures without putting it into context. Prior to the death of Jesus, God's spirit lived in the Holy of the Holies within the Jewish temple. After the death of Jesus, the spirit left the temple and resided within us as followers of Christ. This is a clear example of well-meaning Christians that cannot comprehend God's salvation as a gift obtained by grace. Instead, they want to earn their salvation which cannot be achieved. In the process of trying to earn their salvation, they risk becoming self-righteous like the Pharisees which Jesus confronted.

Why did the smiling fat Buddha statutes become more popular in China and the western world than the skinny Buddha statutes? A cheerful and well-fed-looking statute might cheer you up and give you some hope. In ancient China being chubby was a symbol of good health and wealth. My understanding is that Zen monks had teachings similar to the teachings of the monks in India. In modern times, I would assume it was a marketing strategy for recruitment, but I don't know if they had marketing majors in those days. This would be an interesting research project someday. In the west, I can understand why the smiling fat Buddha is more popular. The fat Buddha looks well-fed and happy, and he stands for good health and wealth which I think is a better appeal to the western mind.

As I mentioned at the beginning of my writing, my purpose is to discover the reasons for the growing interest in Buddhism in the western world. I'll not attempt to be an expert on Buddhism as I have only looked at two books and some articles. For the purpose of my point here I think that will be sufficient. First, he teaches that intentional meditation is the only way to obtain peace and the path to enlightenment with the ultimate goal of reaching the blissful state of Nirvana. There are some teachings regarding the right way to live which will help us on the path to Nirvana. Inherently, the precepts to proper living are remarkably similar to Christian beliefs. For instance, you should not take a life. However, there is openness to interpretation. For example, if you kill a snake that is about to attack your child that would be ok. It appears the precepts are subject to what is acceptable to your culture. Another example is that Buddhists, for the most part, believe abortion is taking a biological life. Buddhism does not seem to argue about how many months after becoming pregnant is abortion considered taking a life. It appears life begins at conception with Buddhism. If you do get an abortion, you are not doomed to hell. Instead, you get bad Karma which will make it harder to reach Nirvana, hopefully, you acquire enough good Karma to overcome the bad. Now, if you get enough bad Karma, you could, after death reincarnate or be reborn as a worm or pig. Another precept is sexual misconduct, but it makes room for cultural differences meaning misconduct is defined by your culture. That makes sense to me. Besides those precepts, greed, and the constant desire for more is a major hindrance to the path leading to Nirvana. There are many examples in this book that shows the evils caused by the love of money.

The Buddha did believe in the law of Karma. Just like Hinduism, after death, a person could come back as an animal or person. In Buddhism, bad or good Karma could affect us and others while we are still alive. For example, a woman goes shopping and leaves the car keys in the car when she goes into the store. While shopping, the car is stolen. When her husband hears of this, he gets angry at her, and a fight ensues. His wife then takes out her frustration on the children. Basically, karma can start a bad chain reaction or a good reaction. Therefore, we should recognize that and create good karma and if possible, not respond to bad Karma. I don't think too many could argue with this principal. I read many chapters on how Buddhism teaches how we treat each other is especially important.

Matthew 7:12 *"Therefore all things whatsoever ye would that men should do to you, do ye even so to them: for this is the law and the prophets"*.Better known as the Golden Rule. This concept appears to have been around in early Confucian times (551-479 BCE). the concept appears to be shared with all the major religions.

The Buddha taught that the source of suffering was within us and could only be eliminated through meditation and proper lifestyle and is part of the process of following the path to Nirvana. He taught to focus on reality and detach yourself from your senses through meditation. The Buddha asked a woman who was grieving because of the loss of a child how she would like it if everyone in a nearby city was her children. She responded joyfully and said yes, she would love to have all those children. The Buddha responded that if that were the case, she would be suffering with grief every day since her children would be dying daily. It appears the Buddha taught that one should love everybody as well as the animals and nature itself. In the abstract, he taught love but not love that is attached to someone you know personally. Therefore, you should try to un-attach to all senses. I can see not being attached with love for my new car or money, but I don't see how that could be done concerning the people I have cared about and loved. Furthermore, I don't think I want to become unattached from those feelings. It is those connections that might be the only thing that makes life worth living and I certainly would not want to block those connections. If terrible grief is the price that I pay for those connections, so be it.

Matthew 22:39 *"And the second I like unto it, thou shalt love thy neighbor as thyself".*

I should add there are verses that explain that the word neighbor is not referring to only the guy next door. Anyone could be considered a neighbor.

John 13:34 *"A new commandment I give unto you, that ye love one another: as I have loved you, that ye also love one another".*

I do not understand why a person would prefer to love mankind on an abstract basis but try to detach oneself from loving on a personal basis. Loving mankind might be great, but it does not seem to be able to replace one on one love.

What is Nirvana? It appears that it is outside the world we know. Perhaps another dimension. Do we have a soul that goes to this blissful place? From what I read it appears we are united or integrated into some cosmic spirit. It appears we are some disembodied entities of some sort being able to exist in a blissful state with a big bonus of not having to be reborn and go through the suffering that comes with life. It sounds good and non-destructive, but I have a different conception of Nirvana. It is called Paradise. As for eliminating suffering from within is certainly a good goal. There are bible verses that might help with suffering such as **Matthew 11:29-30** *"Take my yoke upon you and learn of me; for I am meek and lowly in heart: and ye shall find rest unto your souls. For my yoke is easy, and the burden is light"*. Grant you that is easier said than done but if you can do it, it will help with suffering. At this time, I want to say I like Buddhism. It does not have a history of human sacrifice or monks becoming wealthy from their followers. Also, the Buddha rejected the Rig Veda's along with the Caste system. Buddha taught the law of Karma but taught that a person could reach Nirvana in their life without having to work their way up the social ladder through reincarnation which was different than Hindu teachings. He also accepted women students. In spite of all those good things, I prefer the visual concept of Paradise over Nirvana. At the beginning of this chapter, I quoted some scripture where Jesus was preparing a place for us to go and be with him in heaven someday. I do not know when he will come for us, but this is how he will do it.

1 Thessalonians 4: 16-17 *"For the Lord himself shall descend from heaven with a shout, with the voice of the archangel, and with the trump of God: and the dead in Christ shall rise first then we which are alive and remain shall be caught up together with them in the clouds to meet the Lord in the air and so shall we ever be with the Lord"*. I assume it will be around that time Jesus will take us to the place he had prepared. No matter what your beliefs are, you have to admit, it sounds like a very good ending.

I admit my ending depends on a God that has created everything. Whereas Buddhism does not seem to teach that there is a creator God. It appears that Buddha did not think that the question was important. He told a student that it is better to be ethical than worshiping a God. I am not surprised that Buddha would think that after studying the culture he lived in. Remember, they had many Gods, or as mentioned earlier when one author called them manifestations of God. However, my readings have shown me that some of those manifestations asked for human sacrifice and bride burning. One of their manifestations asked specifically for children to be sacrificed. I can find no record of such atrocities being performed by Buddhists. It appears the Buddha was extremely ethical and moral. It is a fact the Buddha rejected the teachings of the Vedas and the Caste system. A system that was taught in their most sacred Hindu teachings. The Caste system was a form of extreme class suppression and caused much suffering. Because of the culture Buddha lived in, I think, it affected his opinion on the subject of Deity.

As for reincarnation, I believe it is possible, and I believe the bible may support my belief. I have argued this with other Christians because the vast majority of Christians do not believe in reincarnation. In **Matthew 11:14** Jesus says that John the Baptist is *"Elijah who is to come."* It was prophesied that Elijah would return to earth to pave the way for the Messiah Jesus to come and start his ministry. As scripture shows, John the Baptist, was the one who baptized Jesus. If Jesus himself said that John the Baptist was fulfilling the prophesy that Elijah was going to return before the Messiah, I believe Jesus. **Luke 1:17** says that John will go before the Messiah *"in the spirit and* *power of Elijah.*" The Gospel of Mark also says that prophesy of the return of Elijah was fulfilled by John the Baptist. Elijah was supposed to be the one who prepares the way of the Messiah as promised in **Isaiah 40:3.** This was a clear biblical example that reincarnation could be possible.

Other biblical teachings that I think support the possibilities of reincarnation are

2 Peter 3:9 *"The Lord is not slack concerning his promise, as some men count slackness; but is longsuffering to us-ward, not willing that any should perish, but that all should come to repentance".*

Matthew 20: 24-26 *"And again I say unto you, it is easier for a camel to go through the eye of a needle than for a rich man to enter into the kingdom of God. When his disciples heard it, they were exceedingly amazed, saying, "who then can be saved?". But Jesus beheld them, and said, unto them. "With men it is impossible, but with God all things are possible".*

From these scriptures i conclude that if it serves God's purpose, reincarnation is possible. It seems all mysteries have not been explained by the statement "with God all things are possible." Furthermore, reincarnation was believed by many Christians at one time. The belief in reincarnation was declared heresy in 553 AD by the catholic church. Reincarnation was declared heresy by the church because it might be harder to control people and have them blindly obey the church if they think they can get another chance at salvation in the next life. By making the thought heresy the catholic church leaders could get the Inquisition to enforce the church law. The previous chapters tell us what happened to heretics.

The Buddha was a prince, so I assume he was educated. After spending years of meditating, he rejected many of the teachings that prevailed in his culture which, I think, made him an exceptional person. There have been many Buddhas but the first one was the pioneer.

I find that the Buddha teachings did not support the thought of there being an intelligent creator God. In the books I read, Buddhism was very vague on the subject of creationism and the concept of a deity.

FINAL CONCLUSION

I believe the initial growth of Buddhism can be contributed to several things. Buddha rejected many of the prevailing beliefs of his culture. As mentioned earlier, he rejected the prevailing Caste system which created much suffering. Regardless of what Caste system you traditionally belonged to you could be a student of Buddhism. The Buddha believed in The Law of Karma, but he taught that it is possible for a student to reach Nirvana in his or her current life and did not need to work their way up the Caste system by being reborn many times. I am not sure which reason was the main attraction. Was it reaching the blissful state of Nirvana or not having to be reborn countless times? Considering the Caste systems oppressive teachings, it was most likely both factors. For instance, women were taught a good wife had to feed her husband and make sure he was finished before she could eat. I challenge all married men to go home and try that concept out on their wives (only if they have nerves of steel and lack all common sense). I should mention the Buddha did accept women students and nuns. Having rejected the Vedas such things as bride burning and other human sacrifice was also rejected. In my studies, Buddhism has never practiced human sacrifice. The Buddha was from the ruling caste, and he attracted students from the wealthy Caste as well. It was those members that account for the cost of the Buddhist temples that were built. I honestly believe that the early growth of Buddhism was a passive socio-economic revolution against the rules of the Caste system. People were not to even socialize with those in a different Caste. That was deliberate because if friendships in various Caste developed, the disparities in equality might be rejected and be a threat to the ruling Caste. This however is my opinion and is based on my readings and common sense.

The growth of Buddhism in the western world is different. First, secularism has grown tremendously in the western world in the last 50 years for many reasons. The wrongful accusations of Christianity for the atrocities committed. Several of the atrocities have been discussed already yet there are many more which I have not covered as I am avoiding being redundant. I am sure that a study of those atrocities would reveal they were in contradiction to the teachings and examples of Jesus and his Apostles. Some secularists do not want to do anything that might contradict their ideology. This group of people, particularly those in academia and the media have helped to advance a negative image of Christianity. They show examples of a white person doing a hate crime in the name of God and from that call Christians (especially evangelistic

Christian's) racist. When I was young it was considered wrong to stereotype. It appears that these days its OK to stereotype if its against Christians. Yes, there is a small percentage of "proclaiming" Christians that are full of hate but thank God most are not. I say this because I sometimes go to church, and it's integrated as most are these days and what matters to the church members is that we are all brothers and sisters in Christ regardless of color or ethnicity. There is a group of people that do not want to hear this because it contradicts the groupthink they have been promoting for years. I should add that in God's house Republicans, Democrats, blacks, and whites are brothers and sisters in Christ and can still disagree on how the public money should be spent. Politicians will gladly use any narrative if it will get them votes. I think facts show that politicians want power and success so much that they cannot be trusted to be truthful no matter what their political party. I think, most people have a yearning for answers to their spiritual questions. Because of the negativity that Christianity has wrongfully been accused, many people start looking elsewhere for answers to their questions. If you are unhappy with Christianity because of false atrocities and claims of racism, Buddhism appears to be a great alternative. Buddhism has no history of atrocities or racism, and it shares many of the core values and ethics of Christianity. Why do so many people want others to think Christianity is so wrong? It appears they are accomplishing their goal. There are some that might say it is prophesy. Earlier I spoke about the spirit of the Antichrist which entered our world at the death of Jesus. Is that the answer? I do not know. I hope not, because if it is prophesy being fulfilled, it will be unstoppable. All of these things have created an extremely negative image of Christianity leading people to search elseward. There is also atheist in the secular population and gladly say anything that is negative toward Christians. Those atheists do not want a society that offers people freedom of religion. Instead, they want a society that has no religion. Look at China and Russia where the atheistic governments tried to destroy all religions.

Last of all, I would like to mention one other thing that has driven people away from Christianity and that is the traditionally taught concept of Hell. I know when I was growing up, I can remember hearing preachers many times talking about going to hell and spend eternity in this eternal fire and existing in eternal pain. The scriptures do not support that belief, so I do not know why it was taught. Yes, there is an eternal burning lake, but the souls are destroyed and do not burn forever. **Matthew 10:28** says *"And fear not them which kill the body but are not able to kill the soul: but rather fear him which is able to destroy both soul and body in hell"*. Please note the scripture uses the word destroy in the second part and not kill. This scripture shows that a soul is destroyed and does not spend eternity in pain. Even with this less painful concept of hell, it still sounds like a place to avoid. Yes, scripture does say there is a hell where souls will be destroyed but I think there will be far fewer souls destroyed than what most people think. I say this based upon the scriptures and the examples that Jesus and his Apostle gave.

According to the Bible there will be two Judgement days. The first Judgement Day called "the judgment seat of Christ" and will be for those in Christ. Everyone at that judgement will go to heaven but some may have special honors bestowed on them. For instance, if you died a martyr, you get a crown of martyrdom. There are many types of crowns that will be given. I have looked at myself and feel that I will not get any crowns or special honors. Regardless, I will be overjoyed to just be there at the gathering.

The second Judgement Day is for those not in Christ. This judgment is called the "Great White Throne" judgment. Each person will have his works good and bad judged, as well as every idle word spoken. Some will have their souls destroyed in the eternal fire, but I believe most will go to paradise. This opinion is contrary to what many church leaders preach but I think the bible supports my opinion. Here are a few scriptures to support this. **2 Peter 3:9** *"The Lord is not slack concerning his promise, as some men count slackness; but is longsuffering to us-ward, not willing that any should perish, but that all should come to repentance".* This clearly says that God does not want anyone to perish. Early stated was **Matthew 19:26** *"But Jesus looked at them and said, 'with man this is impossible, but with God all things are possible'".* Explaining that even though it looks impossible for a rich man to go to heaven with God all things are possible". Both of these scriptures support my opinion that many of the souls at the 2nd Judgement will have their good works and bad works revealed along with the motives of their hearts and then be pardoned of their sins and allowed to go to heaven. Another bible verse that supports this thought that I have not previously mentioned is **1Timothy 1:12-13** *"And I thank Christ Jesus our Lord who hath enabled me, for that he counted me faithful, putting me into ministry, Who was before a blasphemer, and a persecutor, and injurious: but obtained mercy. Because I did it ignorantly in unbelief"*Before Paul became an apostle, he was arresting Christians and executing them but because of Paul's ignorance, God forgave him and even made him an Apostle. Paul had many extremely bad works but apparently, he had a good heart and well-meaning motives. This makes me think about the many times I have heard someone say ignorance of the law is no excuse. That may be the case in man's court of law, but it seems God will consider a person's ignorance as a defense that can lead to a pardon. Another verse that supports my belief is **Luke 23:34** *"Then said Jesus, Father, forgive them; for they know not what they do. And they parted his raiment and cast lots".* Here is an example where Jesus asked the Father to forgive the people that are brutally executing him. This does not seem like a person that would have billions of souls gather for a final judgement and not consider each person's culture and circumstance before condemning their soul to be destroyed by an eternal fire of hell. As something to consider, I am going to create an example. Let us say the original Buddha shows up at the 2nd Judgement which I suspect he will be incredibly surprised when it happens. In my opinion he was sleeping waiting to be awakened for this event. Every bad thing and good thing he has ever done as well as the motives in his heart will be brought to light. From my research he was not greedy or corrupt and he taught that good morals and ethics should be sought diligently to reach Nirvana. As far as his teachings on those subjects, they are remarkably similar to Christian teachings and I am not surprised since God has written these things in the heart of all men, as mentioned earlier. I could go on and on with many more scriptures, but I think these examples should suffice to support my belief that Jesus will probably give the Buddha a pass into heaven along with many more souls that traditional Christian teachings would have us believe they would go to hell.

I have read that stress and anxiety causes many of our illnesses and unhappiness. Based on that I can see why using the Buddha s meditation technics could be an extremely healthy practice because in the western world we live in a fast paced and goal-oriented culture. If using Buddhism to help unclutter the mind and find some inner peace and discover what is important, by all means do it. I think a person can do that and still be a Christian. Another thing that appeals to many in the western world, is that it comes across as exotic which intrigues people. Last of all, Buddhism has a great symbol. You have got to admit, when you look at the statute of the fat and happy Buddha, you have got to like that guy. The purpose of this writing was to show that true Christianity should not be blamed for atrocities which were performed in the name of God by greedy and power-seeking men of whom many were to be our spiritual leaders.

"That's all Folks"

REFERENCES

The Origins of The Inquisition in Fifteenth Century Spain
By: B. Netanyahu

Confiscation in the Economy of the Spanish Inquisition
By: Henry Kamen

Medieval Christianity
A new History
By: Kevin Madigan

Inquisition, The reign of Terror
By: Toby Green

When Montezuma Met Cortes
By: Matthew Ristal

Cuba
A new history
By: Richard Gott

Where there is Love, there is God
By: Mother Teresa

THE Witchs, Salem, 1692
By: Dan Jones

MANY MANY MANY GODS of HINDUISM
By: Swami Achthananda

No-Nonsense BUDDHISM FOR BEGINNERS
By: NOAH RASHETA

HOLY BIBLE
King James Version

www.ingramcontent.com/pod-product-compliance
Lightning Source LLC
Chambersburg PA
CBHW051712040426
42446CB00008B/852